Jayleen

From

[signature] ♡

Date

February 2021

May you be blessed reading this book & discover your worth in God. Seek Him with all your heart and you will find Him.

He loves you so much ♡
God Bless you!

From Existing to Living:

How to discover your worth in God and live a victorious life.

ANA BAEZ

From Existing to Living

How to discover your worth in God and live a victorious life

Copyright © 2020 by **Ana Baez**

ISBN: 978-1-952098-32-1

Printed in the United States of America. All rights reserved solely by the publisher. This book or parts thereof may not be reproduced in any form, stored in a retrieval system, or transmitted in any form by any means - electronic, mechanical, photocopy. Unless otherwise noted, Bible quotations are taken from the Holy Bible, New King James Version (NKJV) Copyright 1982 by Thomas Nelson, Inc., publishers. Used by permission.

Cornerstone Publishing

A Division of Cornerstone Creativity Group LLC
Phone: +1(516) 547-4999
info@thecornerstonepublishers.com
www.thecornerstonepublishers.com

To contact the author, please follow her on:

Facebook / Ana Baez
Instagram / @iamapprovedbygod
Podcast / Baez Impact Podcast

CONTENTS

Foreword..7

Introduction..9

Chapter One
The Love That God Has For Us..........................15

Chapter Two
The Importance of Surrendering.........................21

Chapter Three
Who Is God?...29

Chapter Four
What To Do To Surrender....................................35

Chapter Five
The Benefits of Surrendering..............................45

Chapter Six
The Consequences of Not Surrendering.............53

Chapter Seven
How Our Disobedience Affects Others..............59

Chapter Eight
Why Do We Feel a Void Without God................63

Chapter Nine
The Things We Seek to Complete Us..................67

Chapter Ten
Why Did God Create Us?......................................71

FOREWORD

Ana Baez is an overcomer. Triumphing over depression, rejection and tremendous hardship, Ana is the perfect candidate to provide readers with insightful tips to living a fulfilled and transformative life. Her voice is one of care and guidance to the lost and lonely. She brings much comfort to the reader to know they're in authentic and capable hands to understand biblical truths about their Christ identity.

From Existing to Living will challenge you to truly evaluate which part of the spectrum you fall. You will learn just how to discern where you are and how to make the transition to living a life full in Christ. This book is recommended to the young believer and to the one who is contemplating changing. To the woman who thought she knew, but had no clue, and is ready to truly discover who she is and her full worth.

Ana's compassion and care for the reader is

reflected off of every page and her accountability to share this message is nothing short of her God given mandate. You can be sure to be enlightened, encouraged and enlivened as you glide from chapter to chapter in this amazing book that is based on pieces of Ana's story, Christian principles, transparency, love and honesty.

By:

Prophetess Asha Mcdermott

The Prophets Keep

INTRODUCTION

There are too many women living out here with no identity. The lack of identity is what causes them to just be in this world to exist and not to actually live. Just because you were born doesn't necessarily mean that you are living. So, you are probably wondering to yourself, "What am I really going to learn in this book? Is this just another Christian book that teaches you how NOT to worry about anything because God is in control?" Or, "is it just another religious book that talks about God but doesn't quite give you the steps to take to actually live a life in victory?"

To answer your questions, it's a no for both. While most Christian books talk to you about the love of God (and I'm not degrading anyone's work), this book will not only help you learn if you are really living or just existing, but it will also give you the steps you must take to be able to live a life of victory. Believe it or not, it is possible. Even in the world we live in today. Most books do not break down the steps that are needed to be able to live in the world that we're living today. My book will provide you with those steps. When I gave my life to Christ, certain things were not told to me right away. I had to learn as I went along and of course, with God's help as well. But I wished someone really took me by the hand and guided me step by step and warned me about certain things that are very important in this walk.

This book isn't about religious rules and traditions. It's about helping you find your true identity so that you can LIVE. It will help you discover things about yourself that you never knew before. It will also help you understand why you were born. It is a simple and easy-to-read book that will help you take the steps necessary to help you live the life you are supposed to live.

So, who is this for?

Let me ask you, do you know if you're really living? If you answered yes then chances are that you're really not. So, you are in the right place. This book is for you if you have no idea why you were born. It's for you if don't really know who you are. It's for you if you don't know what God wants from you while you are here on earth. It's for you if everything that you do is not giving you the results you want. It's for you if you feel that there is a void in your life. It's for you if nothing that you do completes you or satisfies you permanently. Sounds like you?

This book is also for you if you are already a follower of Christ but still feel stuck in your walk. Or you are a new believer but don't know what's the next steps to take. What's the point of giving your life to God if you are still feeling the same way you felt before? Or if you don't even know what to do next to be able to live a victorious life? Well, you're going to learn how to live a life of victory in a chaotic world, who you really are in God and how to live and not only exist in this world. You'll learn how to make a difference with your life and even how to change the lives of your family while living yours the way God intends.

Who is Ana?

More than likely you're saying to yourself, "Ok, that is good and all, but who are you and why should I take your advice?" Well, I am Ana Baez and I am a wife, a mother of three amazing boys, a social media encourager, a praise dancer and the creator of *"Baez Impact Podcast"* where I teach the word of God and share my testimonies in hopes to impact other lives and minister to them on behalf of God. I gave my life to Christ in 2008.

Before I gave my life to Christ, I was living a life of destruction and I didn't know my worth. But I noticed that even after giving my life to Him, I was still doing things I was not supposed to do. Not knowing that it was affecting me spiritually. I was just wasting time doing things that were not productive instead of living life the right way. There was more to life and I had no idea.

So, in the year 2011, I learned more about myself through getting to know God at a personal level. It took me 3 years to finally live. As time went on, I realized the real purpose for my life.

I wanted to share with you the things I did before knowing who God was that led me to consequences that were unimaginable. And why we do the things we do in life and the root of it all. I have been in your shoes. I know exactly how you feel and the many questions you have. This is why you should pay attention to what I'm saying.

What you're going to learn

In order to truly discover your worth in God and live a victorious life, it's vital that we are on the same page. In Chapter 1, I talk to you about the love of God. This was the turning point where I discovered how much God really loved me. There's a reason I begin speaking about His love first. And you'll see why once you begin to read it.

In order for you to fully understand your worth in God and the reason you should say yes to Him, you must know the importance of surrendering. And this is what I talk about in Chapter 2. You will learn exactly why you should surrender and why is it important. But it's not ok to just know about the love of God and the importance of surrendering; you have to also KNOW exactly who you'll be surrendering to. No one wants to surrender to someone they don't know, right? I cover that in Chapter 3; I speak about who God is.

In Chapter 4, I dive in to the steps needed to surrender. You will not be confused at all. They're simple but yet powerful steps. Some people desire to give God an opportunity but don't know where to begin.

In Chapter 5, I speak about your benefit package. Yes, there's a benefit package that comes with this 'yes'! I talk about the benefits you will gain once you surrender. Everyone wants to know the 'why' for everything so in this Chapter, you will find the answers to your questions.

Chapter 6 is about the consequences of not

surrendering. We all know that if we gain benefits when doing right, we also gain consequences when doing wrong. We reap what we sow. I think it's important to know these things to help you make your decision.

In Chapter 7 we'll look at how our disobedience or our 'No' affects others around us. Believe it or not, your decision affects others as well. Many people do not have knowledge of this. Which is why I talk about it because I did not know either.

Have you ever wondered why you feel a void? In Chapter 8 I explain the reason we feel voids in our lives. This is a very important chapter because it will answer most of your questions. Sometimes we do not know why we do the things we do. In this chapter you will realize why you need God.

In Chapter 8, I speak on the things we do to fill that void. I explain why some of those things leave you feeling the same way.

Finally, in Chapter 10, you will read about your purpose here on earth. You will discover exactly why you were born and what you are supposed to do here. You will finally learn how to live and not only exist.

Now that you know what to expect in this book, let's get started! Keep an opened mind…

Chapter One

THE LOVE THAT GOD HAS FOR US

Learn to forgive yourself

Open up your heart to receive God's forgiveness

Value yourself in the process & know your worth

Enjoy God's love for you

Matthew 6:33 "But first and most importantly seek (aim at, strive after) His kingdom and His righteousness (His way of doing and being right- the attitude and character of God), and all these things will be given to you also."

I think I know what made you buy this book. You're most likely curious about the book title! Or you are probably looking for changes in your life. Did you know that it is possible to exist and not be living? As you read this book, you will find out if you're REALLY living and not only existing. Just make sure you stick through the whole book to get a better understanding. Before I gave my life to Christ, I had no idea how much He loved me. Which was the reason why I did the things that I did in my past that led to destruction. I did not know that I was JUST existing and not living! I'll explain. I knew that I was born and that I was here on earth but did not know for what. Perhaps you feel the same way but I promise you that by the time you finish this book, you will know that God loves you and that you were created for more. But not only that, you will know exactly why you are here.

The first time I realized that God did love me was when I heard of what His son Jesus did for me (and you) on the cross. He sacrificed His life and died for our sins to give us eternal life. You're confused? Don't worry about it right now, I will go deeper with this in the following chapters and I will explain it further. But this was the first time I recognized His unconditional love for me. To this day, I still do not know of anyone that would really lay their lives for mine!

From that point on, I never went back to my old life. God has shown me over and over again that He is the one that completes me and that with Him

I shall not lack anything. I learned that things are way better with Him by my side. Even my trials and tribulations. I will also explain this further down the line. God has shown me that I matter to Him. That I was created in His image and likeness to fulfill a purpose here on earth. He has shown me that He can use me for His glory. He has shown me all of these things and much more, through my trials. In every trial there's a lesson to learn. A lesson that helps me grow more and that gets me closer to Him.

2011 was the year that changed my whole life for the better. I didn't know that I would go from bitter, angry, lost, unworthy, wild, promiscuous. To a life of abundance, security, freedom, self-love, comfort, peace and victory. In order to teach women how to surrender to God so that they may discover their worth and live a victorious life, they will need to understand a few things that are very important. I want to talk to you first about the unconditional love that God has for us. I know that it's hard to believe because you probably feel the way I felt before- UNWORTHY! Well, to be completely honest with you, we do not deserve His love and mercy but He still gives it to us. That's how much He loves us! When our children do something wrong, as parents we still love them and care about them. Well, that's the same exact thing with our Father in heaven. God loves us so much that He sacrificed His son, Jesus Christ to die on the cross for my sins and your sins. John 3:16 states "For God so loved the world, that He gave His only begotten Son, so that whoever believes and trusts in Him shall not perish, but have eternal life". This scripture is saying that God gave His ONLY Son to die for US. I don't know of anyone that loves someone so much that they'll sacrifice their child! I wouldn't do it, that's for sure! He sent His Son to die for us to give us eternal life. So that you and I would not perish. Wow! Now, THAT'S real love! Isaiah 54:10 says "For the mountains may be removed and the hills may shake, But My lovingkindness will not be removed from you, Nor will My covenant of peace be shaken," says the Lord who has compassion on you. I love this scripture because it is basically demonstrating to us how much He loves us. He is telling us that EVERYTHING can change or be removed from us but His love for us will never ever change! People and things may change but God never will. Let me take you now to Romans 5:8 where it says "But God clearly shows and proves His own love for us, by the fact that while we were still sinners, Christ died for us". The fact that we are sinners did not stop Christ from dying for us. That's how great His love is for us. I have one more scripture to take you to, although there are many, many more that talks about His love for us. Ephesians 2:4-5 says "But God, being so very rich in mercy, because of His great and wonderful love with which He loved us, even when we were dead and separated from Him because of our sins, He made us alive together with Christ for by His grace – His undeserved favor and mercy- you have been saved from God's judgement." In other words, God is so merciful that now we are justified because of the sacrifice on the cross. We have been acquitted from judgement. Our debt have been canceled, paid! Now that you've read these scriptures, are you convinced yet that God loves you so much? If not, don't worry about it because by the time you reach the end of this book, I promise you that you will be convinced. God shows us His mercy on a daily basis and at times we don't even realize it. What I love about the mercy of God is that the bible states that His mercies are new every single day. Not just one day or two. But EVERY single day God gives us a new opportunity to get it right. This means that if you sin the day before and you ask God to forgive you the next day and you truly feel remorse about it and repent, then He will forgive you right away. And do you want to know what's the most amazing thing of it all? That when

He forgives you, He will not remember it or even bring it up again. This is just one example of the many things He does to show us His mercy.

When I began to walk with God, I realized that the world does not offer me any good thing for eternity. I learned that I was seeking the things I was lacking in all the wrong places. I didn't know that what I needed was right in front of me. God.

Walking with God and really getting to know Him causes your mentality to shift. You can now see things different because your spiritual eyes have been opened. Before knowing who God was, I did not know my true identity. Nothing made sense to me. I always felt like something was missing and that I was created for more. Just didn't know how to find out. Can you relate? You will not even believe the things I've had to endure to finally give my life to God.

Chapter Two

THE IMPORTANCE OF SURRENDERING

In this chapter you will read about surrendering but I also want to talk a little bit about submission because people often confuse these two words.

I remember cringing at the word 'submission' before. Me? Submitting? Never! Not Ana! It always scared me and made me feel like I'd lost control of my life. After so many crazy things happening in my life, I finally realized that I did not know how to run my own life. I needed help from God. And I still remembered how it felt! Keep reading to find out what happened in my life that led me to say "I give up God. Take control". If you're asking yourself why do you need to surrender to God, I don't blame you. I was there too. I did not know the benefits of surrendering to God and neither did I know about His love for me while I was still a sinner. But in this book, you will read about my story and the things that I had to endure for lack of not knowing who God was. I want you to be aware of the things that I wasn't aware of.

Romans 12:1 says "Therefore I urge you, brothers and sisters, by the mercies of God, to present your bodies [dedicating all of yourselves as a living sacrifice, holy] and well-pleasing to God, which is your rational act of worship". This scripture warns us with urgency to live a pleasing life before God. This is an act of worship. To submit means to give up completely on your own will for the will of a higher authority. Which is God in this case. I am living proof that doing things and making decisions according to my will, got me into a lot of trouble. Which is the reason why I am passionate about writing this book.

I want women to know their worth and to know of a God that loves us so much that even in our messes, He sees us worthy. That's what He did with me. He saw me dirty and took me and cleaned me up! He washed me with His precious blood. I am still a sinner now. The only difference is that I now recognize that I am a sinner that needs Jesus every day. I now see that apart from Him, I cannot do anything. Now I do things according to His will and not my own. Back then I was a sinner that was completely lost. I was a sinner that did not know needed a Savior. Walking around existing but not living. Lacking an identity. I don't want that for you. So please stay with me till the end of this book. Make sure you read every word carefully and meditate on it. This is my life, a real story. It's not fiction. I want to talk to you about the gift of free will. You're most likely asking yourself "what gift??" Yes, God has given us all a gift! Well many gifts if you ask me. But let's focus on this one. I want to talk about this because I want you to know that surrendering to God is a choice. God does not and will never force anyone to surrender to Him. He is that much of a gentleman that He does not forces His way into your heart. He simply waits patiently for you to open up the door for Him. He will simply knock and wait, knock and wait, knock and wait… until you respond. God tells us in His word what to do to have a blessed and fruitful life.

A life in abundance. Eternal life with Him if we surrender. But He also tells us what happens if we choose not to surrender. He gives us the option to choose between life and death. Yes, I said life and death. When we surrender to God, we have eternal spiritual life. When we choose not to surrender, we have eternal spiritual death. This is why the bible states that He gave us the gift of free will. We can choose the path we want. But we cannot say that we never knew about anything when He has left His word. It is all written there. I urge you to choose to surrender so that you may have life. I was dead for so many years and did not even know it. That's why I say that I was just existing. God wants us to also LIVE. To surrender to anyone is hard. I get it! But I think it's harder when we do not know who we are surrendering to and why. In this book you will find the answers to your questions. So, there are no excuses.

Before I continue, I want to explain to you the difference between surrendering and submitting. In order for you to surrender to God, you must first submit to Him. I'll tell you why. There's a huge difference between these two words. They sound almost the same but they're not. Submitting is a choice and it is when we are willing to do something consciously. Surrendering is something that just happens. That's why I say that you must first CHOOSE to submit to God's will before the surrendering occurs. Surrendering to God will follow right after submission. Keep this in mind.

So, let's go back to why it is so hard for most of us to submit to the will of God. I'll mention just one reason I had a hard time before. If you are an independent person or if you are a single mother like I was for many years, you will have a hard time submitting. Why? Because when you're used to doing things on your own for so long, you will feel that you don't need anyone's help. This was my exact mentality before knowing who God was. But the truth is that we cannot do anything at all without the help of God. No matter how we try to put it. Everything you are doing and who you are is because of God. He is the creator of all things. Aside from many other reasons, this was the main reason for me.

Now I am completely dependent on God because I know that He knows best and only wants best for me. I know Him and have a personal relationship with Him. This is why I tell you that you must first know who He is. It'll be easier because you will trust Him. When we meet people, we spend time with them and create a bond and a relationship to get to know them, and THEN we'll learn to trust them. So, it's the same exact thing with God. Once you begin to trust Him, you'll be able to submit and eventually surrender. The trust will definitely come because He will show you that you can absolutely trust Him.

Like I stated in the previous chapter, I was seeking what I was lacking in all the wrong places. I kept doing that for years! But one thing I noticed was that at the end of it all, I still felt the same! Empty, miserable, bitter, angry, and confused. I was so tired of doing things that made me happy for the MOMENT. I was tired of living a life that put a temporary smile on my face. And I was tired of depending on certain things or people to make me happy. I wanted and was desperate to feel inner and everlasting joy. I no longer wanted to allow people to determine my happiness. I wanted full control of my own happiness. And this is why I decided to surrender to God. I had heard good things about Him and wanted to experience it for myself. I was on a mission of finding out if He was really who people say He was.

You're probably asking yourself, "well, how do I know if God is calling me"? Let me tell you how I knew that God was waiting on me to surrender my life to Him. Again, everything that I was doing left me with a void. So, I wanted to try something different. I remember attending a church and feeling something I've never felt before. It was a feeling of security, peace, and love. As the Pastor preached my heart wanted to burst out of my chest. Tears rolled down my face and I didn't know why.

I remember different people always inviting me to church or someone would always talk to me about

God. I also remember me trying to hide from these people because that's not what I wanted. But when I finally attended church for the very first time back in 2008, it was an unexplainable feeling. A feeling I wanted to keep forever. That's when I knew deep in my spirit that God was knocking at my door. I just felt it! Wait until you read about how interesting God is- He is full of surprises all the time. He is an intentional God!

CHAPTER THREE

WHO IS GOD?

You've probably heard many crazy stories out there about who God is. For example, like there is more than one God, there is no God, that God is a woman, that the universe and the stars are God, etcetera. Well, you don't have to wonder anymore. This was a question I always asked myself before knowing who God really was. I didn't believe what people would say about Him until I got to know Him myself personally. There are so many characteristics of who God is. I will try naming just a few names that describes Him. So that way you know who you're submitting to. How can you submit to a person if you don't even know them, right? But you don't have to take it completely from me. After reading the book, seek Him yourself and you will see how good He is. I guarantee you that YOU WILL NEVER GO BACK! He is the Great I Am because He is and always will be, He is Jehovah Jireh meaning Provider, He is Prince of Peace because He is the only one that can give us peace that surpasses all understanding in ANY circumstance, He is Jehovah Nissi because He always Reigns in Victory, He is ABBA meaning Father, He is The Bread of Life because He is Life- the bread that will never make us hunger again, He is Yahweh meaning God, He is the Fountain of Living Water because we will never thirst again and He will never run out, and so much more. John 14:6 says Jesus said to him, "I am *the way*, and *the truth*, and *the life*. (emphasis mine) No one comes to the Father except through me". And we see in Revelation 22:13 that is says "I am the *Alpha* and the *Omega*, the *first* and the *last*, the *beginning* and the *end*". (emphasis mine)

I love each name because just by hearing them, you can feel the love He has for each and every one of us. Have you ever heard of the Holy Trinity? Perhaps you have but never really understood. Let me explain. The word *Tri* means 'three'. The Trinity of God consists of the Father, the Son, and the Holy Spirit. But they are all ONE God. Before I go into the functions of each person of the trinity, let me first explain to you who is the Holy Spirit. So that you can have a better understanding. When we give our lives to Christ, the Holy Spirit comes to dwell inside of us. This means that the Spirit of God (enabling power of God) which is the Holy Spirit is inside of us to guide us, comfort us, help us in times of trouble, teach us new things, reveal the plans of the Father to us and convict us. This is such a privilege! So, going back to the functions or role of each person of the Holy Trinity; The Father comes first. He is the Source, the Sender and the (Planner). The Son comes next. He accomplishes the Father's plan in our lives. (Accomplisher) And then comes the Holy Spirit that will help us walk in that plan and apply salvation. (Applier). What an awesome team! Yes, it is called the trinity but they're all ONE God. **Please note: We do NOT have 3 Gods*** I want you to envision a triangle. At the top of the triangle is the Father because He is first, then on the left bottom side is the Son, Jesus and then at the right bottom side is the Holy Spirit and in the very center of the triangle is GOD. Because it's only one God. God is Sovereign. He is above all! He is the supreme authority and everything is under His control. Colossians 1:16-17 states that "For by Him all things were created, in heaven and on earth, visible and invisible, whether thrones or dominions or rulers or authorities – all things were created through Him and for Him". And He is before all things, and in all things hold together. This includes US as well. How amazing!! I'm going to give you the steps in what to do to submit to God. I hope that all of these things did not overwhelm you. My desire is for you to completely understand who God is and the process we must go through. I don't ever want to sugar coat anything and make it seem like everything will be paradise if you give your life to Christ. Truth is that the trials will not go away. But you will have a God that will be with you forever and He will help you bear the trials. When you don't have God, the trials are unbearable. Trust me, I know! I went through them for years without Christ. Before I continue on to giving you the steps you need to take, I need to tell you something that I notice people always say but it never works. If you're saying to yourself "I'm not ready now but when I'm ready, I'll give my life to Christ". I have news for you. YOU WILL NEVER BE READY! Yes, you read that right. That moment will never happen. You just have to make that decision and that's that. Go straight into it, blindly. I always tell people that they will never feel ready. The devil will always fight you with everything when he sees that you want to give your life to Christ. So why not just do the total opposite of what he wants you to do? The steps you need to take to be saved will shock you! These steps will also help you build a *personal relationship* with God. So take notes! Many people make it look like a project or mission but there's one main thing God looks for in us when we say yes to Him. Keep reading to find out what that is. I can already hear you say "That's all"?

Chapter Four

WHAT TO DO TO SURRENDER

Love God above all

Invite Him DAILY into your life

Value yourself

Enjoy your relationship with God

So, here it is. The moment that I said yes to God! I remember it was almost 10 years ago. I'll be honest, this day wasn't planned by me. It was an orchestrated moment planned by God Himself! When the moment happened, which I'll be telling you about soon, I remember feeling things I've never felt before. My heart wanted to come out of my chest and tears just rolled down my cheeks as I felt God's presence all over my body. I felt a warm sensation, as if God was telling me "Here

I am Daughter". The bible states that if we want to accept Christ and be saved, we must:

1. Confess.

Confess with our mouth that Jesus is Lord and that He died on the cross for our sins. Once we confess that out loud, we are saved! After confessing that we must also:

2. Ask God to forgive our sins.

God will always forgive you but ONLY when you repent of your sins. To repent is to turn away from your sins and to feel complete remorse. And as I mentioned before, the Holy Spirit then dwells inside of us. Now we are saved, forgiven, and have the Spirit of God living inside of us at all times. Which means that we will never be alone again. He guide us and help us.

Do you know why some people do not feel ready or worthy to walk with God? Because they feel like they're not perfect yet. They think that once they give their life to Christ, they need to cut the bad people off, stop doing this and stop doing that. That will only get them overwhelmed and turn them away from God. So, what am I saying with this? Yes, you will change BUT only the Holy Spirit helps you change your way of living and thinking. It's a process. **All you need is a willing heart.** By having a willing heart, you're giving the Holy Spirit permission to work in you. That is why He is living in the inside of us. To help us on the way. God knew that we wouldn't be able to do it on our own. So, if you're thinking that YOU need to make all these changes, it won't happen without the help of the Holy Spirit. Once we decide that we will be living for God, our jobs is to build a personal relationship with Him. This comes with time. But you are the one in control of how deep and intimate your relationship with Him will be. It all depends how much time you are willing to invest. Many do not come to Christ because they begin to think about religion and its law. It's about developing a relationship with your Creator. And this relationship does not only happen in church but outside of church. This relationship develops in our homes, behind closed doors. Are we still going to seek Him out of church? Or are we simply Sunday Servants? God wants complete devotion to Him. This means including Him in your every day lives. He wants to be involved in every small thing to the biggest. But again, He looks for how willing our hearts are. We must read the word of God so that we may know the character of God. You will not know who God is if you don't read the bible. No matter how many times you hear someone preach about Him. We must also pray at all times. Now, this is when many people get confused. I hear some people say "Well I don't know how to pray and for how long". So, because they feel this, they will not pray. Let me tell you something about prayer and take notes. Prayer is simply communication with God. It is a conversation with our Father. People make it so complicated and it really isn't. God wants to hear from you. He wants you to tell Him everything you feel because what concerns you, concerns Him as well. More than you think! Yes, He does know it all but He wants a relationship with you. This is why prayer is very vital in the walk with God. God will speak to you through prayer and you will feel His amazing presence. How do I begin? You may ask. What do I say to Him? Speak to Him about everything you feel. And it's important to be completely honest with Him. He already knows your heart and every thought that runs through your head so might as well be honest. When I first prayed to God about 9 or 10 years ago, I felt crazy and silly because I felt as if I was talking to myself. This is going to happen. But do not allow it to stop you from praying. As time goes on and the more you pray, you will become aware of His presence and even feel His love, so tangible. Even when you feel like you're talking alone, remember that He is actually right there next to you. Just picture Him there with you. My relationship with God began to develop through prayer. I'm going to be completely transparent with you because many don't talk about this after someone gets saved and I think it should be spoken about. A battle begins to happen right after salvation. Yes, a spiritual battle. A battle between the flesh (your desires, your will) and the Spirit (God's will for your life). The flesh will always go against the Spirit. Remember, you've been living for a certain amount of years doing things your way. So, you go from doing things your way and living the way you want to, to living for God and doing things His way. So, what do we do when this happens? We ask God every day through prayer, to help us *die to ourselves*. This means to die to our wants, our desires, our will. Living in the Spirit means to live according to God's will or how God intends for us to live. This is a totally different world for us. It sounds complicated but it is doable. God will help you through this process so don't stress yourself out about it. When babies are born, they are born not knowing a thing. The parents' job is to teach them how to walk, talk, and everything else. There's a process that babies must go through and it's the same with us. God is our Father and He will teach us how to live according to His will because He knows that we're new at this. We go from drinking milk to eating solid food. From baby Christians to mature ones. The maturity level in your life is up to you. How much time you invest in your relationship with God. The devil has this bad habit of making us feel guilty when we are not perfect. God is not looking for you to be perfect because we never will. This guilt will make us feel terrible and it will keep us from seeking God because we feel unworthy to do so. This is called *Condemnation* and it comes from the devil. His goal is to make you feel so guilty that you stop seeking God. But *Conviction* comes from God. Conviction is the work of the Holy Spirit in your life. It allows you to see yourself as God sees you. Totally unable to save yourself. God brings conviction to us with love. This is what I call correction from God. He corrects us because He loves us and want what's best for our spiritual life. So, there's a major difference between these two words. The enemy will always try to confuse you and make you feel like it is God that is condemning you. So, now that we got that out of the way, let's get back to the steps needed to stay in Christ and grow in Him. The next thing to do is to:

3. Take time to read the Bible.

This is the word of God. I understand if you feel like it's complicated to comprehend. I get it, I was there. I always recommend the NIV (New International Version) or the AMP (Amplified Version) because it helps you understand it better. The AMP has helped me a lot. The bible is what transforms your life and your mind. It will LITERARLY transform you! But only if you open it to read it and study it. The Holy Spirit will guide you, help you understand, and will enlighten your understanding. Just ask Him for help before reading and He will. Make sure to have an opened heart to receive the promises of God for your life. I call the bible "Love Letters" from God. The word of God is alive and it is a book of wisdom and directions. The answers to all your questions are in that book. Many say that they don't believe in the bible because it was "written by man". Yes, it was. But all inspired by God. The bible will tell you what to do and what not to do in this walk. There's no excuses. The bible will help you in so many trials. It will bring comfort, peace, encouragement, joy, and so on. It is a lamp unto our feet and a light unto our path. (Psalm 119:105) It will guide us in everything. It has transformed my life tremendously and to this day I still read it and study it every day. It's a must! It is spiritual nourishment. Food for your soul. When we do not eat in the natural, we do not have the nourishment our bodies need to be able to function properly. We starve and if we stay without eating for a very long time, we will die. Same goes with the bible in our lives. It is our daily bread. If we do not read it, we will die spiritually. The bible is very powerful because it is the weapon against the devil. The word of God is what's needed to defeat the enemy in your life. In Matthew 4:1-11 Jesus was tempted by the devil in the wilderness. The way Jesus would respond to the devil was using the word of God. That is how he was able to flee. When the devil comes to tempt you, use the word. The word of God is sharper than a two-edged sword. It will penetrate and cut deeply. That's how much power the word has. And I am living proof that it is alive! God speaks to us through the bible. When you choose not to read the bible, you are only making yourselves targets to the devil. You become vulnerable to him. It will be easy for the devil to deceive you because you would not know what comes from God and what doesn't. One of the ways to get to know God, is through the bible. But if you don't read it how will you be able to decipher which voice is the enemy's and which is God's? That's why it's important to read the word of God. We will eventually become cold and die spiritually if we don't. The bible was written by 35 different Authors like Moses, Paul, and Timothy, to name a few. They were all moved and empowered by the Holy Spirit. Some were prophets and some were apostles. But they were all inspired by God. Another question people ask me a lot about the bible is how do they read it or where do they begin. I was also there in the beginning. I suggest getting one of the two versions I mentioned previously and begin with Genesis and then go on to the Book of John. The book of Genesis tells you how the world was created, how we were created, and how sin came about. The book of John speaks on Jesus ministry and who He is. This book will allow you to understand further who Jesus is and what His ministry was all about. The other thing that is needed to help us build a relationship with God is:

4. Pray.

And we've already discussed the importance of prayer. The last thing and MOST important thing is to have:

5. A Willing Heart.

This will allow God to work in you and in your character. This is telling God "Here I am. Change me". This is being opened to changes.

Let me ask you something- Do you know that surrendering to God brings benefits to you and others? When you apply for a job, they offer you benefits if you get the job done. And if some jobs do not offer benefits, you will not take it. Well, what if I told you that there's no way you will turn down Jesus' offer for you once you find out who He is. Now, please do not misunderstand me. I'm not saying to seek the hand and not the face. But wait till you read what's in your benefit package!

CHAPTER FIVE

THE BENEFITS OF SURRENDERING

I can recall a time I asked myself "Why am I even here"? "What is the point of all of this"? Without realizing the benefits that were awaiting me from giving my life to Christ. I had no idea what God had in store. Not only for me but for my family as well. When I surrendered to God, an exchange of thoughts and emotions were made. I gave God the ones that were harmful to my spirit in exchange for His. He gave me peace for misery, love for anger, security for fear, joy for bitterness, life for death, mercy for condemnation. There are benefits in surrendering to God, otherwise He would not ask us to do it. Everything that God ask us to do is for our own good. Aside from MANY benefits we gain, let me first begin with the mind. I want to start speaking on the mind because it was the first thing that changed for me. And then my actions followed. When I gave my life to Christ, I began to seek a personal relationship with Him. Now, I will be completely transparent with you. This did not happen for me immediately. It was a process. But I did have a willing heart to change and really get to know God on a personal level. As time went by, I became closer to God. I would read the Bible every day and attend Bible Study weekly. This was just the beginning of my relationship with Him. During this process, my mind started to change. God was renewing every thought. I noticed the change in the things I would think about. They went from negative to positive thoughts. Even if someone would say something to offend me, my immediate response was to show them love. To try to understand why they were behaving this way. It was no longer me wanting to retaliate or fight. I now had the mind of Christ. I began to think like Him. My mind was transformed and spending time reading the Bible is what did it. I will talk further about this in the following chapters.

Your mind and how you see things, will change. This is why it's very important to study the word of God. It begins there! Before I came to Christ, I had a very negative mind. Every thought was hopeless and negative. As I began to get closer to God, my mind and thoughts started to change. And this is very important because when you change your thoughts, your actions follow right after. My mind was changing day by day and so were my actions. People that knew me for a very long time, noticed the change in me. That's how it's supposed to be. You're supposed to stand out and be different when you give your life to Christ. You're not supposed to blend in with the rest. And if you do, you're doing something wrong in your walk. We are supposed to reflect God in everything that we do. Even in the way we speak. Another thing that happens is that your faith increases. Faith comes by hearing the Word of God. Before coming to Christ, I had no faith. But as time went on and my relationship grew deeper, so did my faith. Faith is basically believing God. That everything that's written in His word is true. That's faith. Believing in something you don't see yet with your natural eyes. The word of God says that in this walk we must "Walk by Faith and not by Sight". In other words, to have faith even when you don't see what you want to see with your natural eyes. We must see with our spiritual ones. When we have God in our lives, we can handle every trial. He promises in His word that He will always be with us and that He will never leave us nor forsake us. He never said that we will not have trials and tribulations. He did say that He will be with us through them all. Before I had God in my life, I went through every trial afraid, upset, overwhelmed, helpless, and sad. It felt like I couldn't handle the issues I had. And that's because I was doing it with my own effort. Now that I have God in my life, I know that I can bear every trial because He walks with me and gives me of His strength. So, trials are easier with God if we lean on Him and not on our own understanding. Another benefit we have in opening our hearts to God is that when we do, our families also benefit from it. Let me start with your children. Proverbs 22:6 says to "Train up a child in the way he should go: and when he is old, he will not depart from it." They are secured in Christ. They are witnessing the change in you as well. We have Christ dwelling in our homes with us. There will be a shield of protection over them wherever they go. God will guide and direct their steps. All because you are serving Him. He says, "If you take care of what's mine (the relationship with Him), I will take care of what's yours (our families). Another scripture that describes the benefits our children will gain is Deuteronomy 4:39-40 that says "Therefore know and understand today, and take it to your heart, that the Lord is God in the heavens above and on the earth below; there is no other. So you shall keep His statutes and His commandments which I am commanding you today, so that it may go well with you and with your children after you, and so that you may live long on the land which the Lord your God is giving you for all time." No need to explain this one, it's self-explanatory.

Our family (apart from our children) will also benefit from our decision. How so? You are a living testimony to your family. No one knows you better than they do. They knew you in your past. You will be "preaching" to them with your life without really saying a word. Sometimes, you will be the only bible some people will read. So, picture yourself as a bible in two feet. When they begin to see the changes in you, they will want to also experience that. When you give your life to Christ, you will also be breaking generational curses. Chains will be broken in your family because of your decision. And last but not least, you will have ETERNAL life when you say yes to God. Eternal life in heaven when you pass away. There is a heaven and a hell and they are real. When you give your life to Christ, you will live with God in eternity. When we decide to say no to God, we live an eternal life in hell with the devil. And I don't know about you, but that's too scary for me! I rather be with God in eternity. John 10:27-28 says "My sheep listen to my voice; I know them, and they follow me. I give them eternal life, and they shall never perish, no one will snatch them out of my hand". This scripture is saying that those that didn't know God before, were like a lost sheep without a shepherd. Now that we have found Him, we know Him and recognize His voice and we can follow Him. And that He gives us eternal life. John 5:24 says "Very truly I tell you, whoever hears my word and believes him who sent me, has eternal life and will not be judged but has crossed over from death to life". In this scripture, Jesus is telling us that whoever hear His word and believes in the Father (that sent Him), will have eternal life. This is how we become saved and free from condemnation. We cross over from death (the world) to life (In Christ). And the last scripture I want to talk to you about is John 6:51. It says "I am the living bread which came down from heaven: if any man eat of this bread, he shall live forever: and the bread that I give is my flesh, which I will give for the life of the world. If anyone eats of this bread he will live forever." To summarize it for you, it is saying that Jesus died on the cross for us. To give us eternal life. This is what He meant by flesh. His body. If we taste how good He is, we will live forever because we will never be hungry again. What great benefits are these!

Now that we went over the benefits of saying yes

to God, let's go over the consequences of saying no. You DO NOT want to stop here! You've reached the most important part of the book. This is what's going to help you make your decision. You will now be able to compare the benefits with the consequences and determine which one you prefer. Because remember, you have free will.

CHAPTER SIX

THE CONSEQUENCES OF NOT SURRENDERING

I remember clubbing one cold winter and instead of going home right after, I ended up in someone's bed. There were actually many of these nights. I was so drunk that I barely remembered anything. I remember waking up and feeling afraid many times because I barely knew the man I was laying right next to. I had no idea that the consequences to these actions were going to catch up to me the way they did. Just as surrendering to God brings benefits, NOT surrendering also brings consequences. Disobedience to God shows in our actions. Before knowing God, every action I took was not one pleasing to Him. I would speak too quick before thinking and did not care who it would damage. Also, living the promiscuous life being another one. I was spiritually dead!

The consequences that I had to face for the promiscuous life were men talking bad about me and looking down at me. I also had to deal with some hurtful words being told to me about my character and integrity. I had no self-respect. I can't believe I'm going to talk about this but I want you to understand the severity of my promiscuous life. I remember a time I was waiting in a clinic's waiting area to get tested for sexually transmitted diseases. I felt so anxious and afraid to get the test results because I knew how wild I was. I knew that there was a great possibility that my tests would come back positive for HIV. I can still remember the nurse calling me inside to get my vital signs and telling me that I needed to wait at least 15 minutes to calm down because my blood pressure was way too high. I was so nervous that it showed in my vital signs. I remember my palms sweating as I waited for the HIV results. There was always a sigh of relief after the words "It's Negative". There was also a time I received a phone call from the clinic and I remember a nurse telling me that one of the test came back positive and that there was really no cure. My body and knees began to shake and I felt weakness all over my body! Turned out that they had the wrong patient. Whew! What a wake-up call! It should have been a wake-up call I should say. You would think that this would've stopped me. Well, it didn't. I continued being promiscuous without a care in the world. These actions also led me to have several abortions. I don't have shame speaking about these things because God changed me. This is how amazing and loving God is; that He loves us unconditionally. He forgave me for all of it because I repented and asked for forgiveness. Of course I would've love to do things way different but I have no regrets because these actions led me to God. God saved my life over and over again and He wants to save yours as well. And these are just a few examples of what I had to face for not being obedient to God. I was always going clubbing every weekend and drinking. I drank so much sometimes that I did not even know how I got home or who's apartment I would end up in. I also smoked a lot of weed in my teenage years. But that all changed when something was put inside of it that made me almost kill myself. I began to hallucinate and I almost threw myself out of a window. That was the scariest thing ever!! I thought that I was going to die! Again…consequences! Again… God saved me!

Our trials and tribulations are harder without God. Why? Because there's no guidance, direction, peace, security, faith, or joy. When we face things in life without the God that knows it all, we will go through them in distress. Feeling hopeless and afraid. That's what I was feeling in every trial. Let me take you down this memory lane real quick of a big trial I went through without God. Back in 2009 I ended up in a shelter with my two children that were ages 7 and 6 months. Although I did give my life to God in 2008, I still had not developed a personal relationship with Him yet. A lot happened in that process and I went through everything in desperation and confusion. I had no idea what I was going to do with two small children in a shelter that was so far away from where I was before. I did not know anyone there. There were many nights where I would cry myself to sleep. But I'm sure if I knew then what I know now about God, I would've went through that trial gracefully and at peace. Not knowing God will make your trial more difficult to bear. I was actually opening the doors for the demons to enter my life AND my body! I've been talking so much about this devil and this enemy so let me explain to you who he is. The bible states that the devil was once an angel. Yes, God created him. His name in heaven was 'Lucifer' which means "light-bringer" or "light bearer". He was the one in charge of the worship. The angel of music. He was the most beautiful angel and had a big role in heaven. But one thing happened with his character that made

God cast him out of heaven. He became jealous of God and arrogant. He wanted to be like Him. He thought he was better than the other angels because he was the most beautiful one. He became rebellious towards God. Because of this behavior, he was casted out of heaven and he took with him one-third of the angels. (Revelation 12:4). Those angels are now his demons. They work under him. He was casted out into the world. Now his name is Satan and he also has a plan for your life. His plans for your life is to kill, steal, and destroy everything that God has for you. He hates us because God created us and we look like Him. When he sees you, he sees God. Because we were created into God's image and likeness. And because he hates God, he hates us too. He doesn't want you to serve God because he want you to die spiritually and live with him in eternity. In hell, miserable. God says in His word that His plans for your life is to prosper you and to give you a future and a hope. That's the plan I rather go with! Your actions will follow your disobedience as well. Your actions will not be wise because you are not living a pleasing life to God. The devil wants you to live a life that will destroy you. Remember, that is his plan for your life. When we do not have God, our thoughts are also not pleasing to God. We will live a life full of negativity. The majority of the times we think that our disobedience only affects us and that's it. Nope. It affects others too believe it or not. Find out how, in the next chapter.

CHAPTER SEVEN

HOW OUR DISOBEDIENCE AFFECTS OTHERS

Imagine yourself inside of a train and you are in a rush to get to work and someone presses the emergency break abruptly? Now you have no other choice but to wait for assistance along with everyone else in the train because of someone else's action. Now you get to work super late. And all of this because of one person's action. It's like they have control over your day at that moment. Well, this is what it looks like when our disobedience affects others around us. You probably do not know that your disobedience to God affects others as well, especially your family. I did not know this either! But you are lucky to be reading this book because now you know. Before I gave my life to Christ, my family did not know much about God. What does this have to do with my disobedience?

I'll explain. What God does is that He chooses a person from each family to be the anchor of the family. To make a difference and lead them the path to God. I did not know that God had me in mind to be that anchor for my family. Me? A sinner?

If I did not choose to give my life to Christ, my family would probably still be lost as well. I'm not taking all the credit and saying that because of ME they are where they are. Absolutely not! God gets all the glory and honor for that. What I am saying is that God used me to bring them to His feet. When we choose to disobey God and not surrender to Him, our family pays for it as well. How can they know of a God that saves if they don't see a living example of His love? How can they see if God is real if they don't see Him through you? How can they be saved if no one is speaking to them about God? Yes, they can get to know God through someone else but people change faster when they see their own family member change. It's now more personal to them. Now they want to know why and how you're changing. Now they begin to want a taste of what you are experiencing. Now they feel more courageous to try God out. That's the difference! Be their example! Be that anchor for your family! You will see God's hand over them as they see you changing your ways for the better. It feels like you're making someone pay for your actions. The same way our decision of saying yes to God benefits our families, saying no to God affect them as well. Your children will also pay for your disobedience. Generational curses will follow them and their children and their children's children and so on. This is what the enemy wants; to keep you and your family in bondage. Your disobedience will even affect others around you. People that don't really know you personally or your friends. You will not be able to witness to others about the love of God. I always say that there is a soul assigned to each one of us. What does that mean. Some people are waiting for you so that they can know God and be delivered. Some one somewhere is waiting for their prison doors to open and you have those keys. Have you ever wondered why we do what we do? There must be a reason. Yes, there is.

Chapter Eight

WHY DO WE FEEL A VOID WITHOUT GOD

The only good memory I have of my father before he passed away 11 years ago, was the one when I was 4 years old laying down with him. I remember his arms wrapped around me as I slept. I can still smell him. The smell of a father. This was the only time I can say that he was being my daddy. When he began making the decisions that he did, he created in me a void. I grew up not knowing who I really was. The feeling of confusion and uncertainty led me towards the path of destruction. I desperately needed to seek something to make me feel better of who I was. When we do not know God on a personal level, we do not have an identity. Or better yet, we do not KNOW who we really are. Before coming to the feet of Christ I was completely lost. This is why I always felt a void- because I did not have God in my life to lead me. I was depending on my own strengths and efforts to be successful in everything. But it all failed!

When we do not know who we are in Christ, we will not make the right decisions in life because we do not know who we were created to be. But when we meet God, we will begin to see ourselves the way He sees us. We will walk in our purpose and be guided by God every step of the way. No matter what you do, that void will always be there. God created us so that we may serve Him. And if we do not live a life that He created us for, we will feel that void. Serving God fills that void because we are doing as God intends. We do everything according to His will. Everything that we do will be pleasing to Him. We also feel a void when we lack knowledge of who God is. This is called "spiritual blindness". We cannot understand the things of the spirit or even who God is because we do not know Him. All we know is what we know since we were born (if we were born out of church). When we give ourselves to God, our spiritual eyes become opened. The

scales from our eyes are removed. This happens as we spend time with Him, especially in studying the bible. When we aren't serving God, there is something blocking our vision. There is spiritual darkness. But when we have God, we have light! He is the light of the world and if we are His followers, the bible states that we are to also be the light of the world. This means that wherever we are and whomever we encounter, there will be light in the midst because we are there and God's spirit lives in us. Spiritual blindness happens when we are in the world, meaning if we aren't serving God, truth is that we are serving the enemy. The bible states that if we are not following Christ, we are enemies of God. And I know that sounds a little harsh and hard to believe but it is the truth. There is nothing good in the enemy, he is all darkness. Now, THIS is where it gets more interesting! You're about to read about the crazy things I did for lack of not knowing who God was and because I lacked a father figure in my life.

Chapter Nine

THE THINGS WE SEEK TO COMPLETE US

Wild parties, drunken nights, and sex were my escape from reality. I remember the feeling of a hung over night, the room spinning as I grinded on a man at the dance floor, my head in the toilet as I puked everything I drank hours before, the feeling my body felt when a man would tell me "I love you". After every night of "having fun" I was still the empty, miserable, lost Ana I was that morning and the day before and the day before that. When we do not know who we were created to be, we seek things that are temporary to fill that void. I say temporary because I was always feeling the same afterwards. Nothing was satisfying me completely. Before I get to my story, let me first explain to you how the void forms in us. Besides not knowing God, things in our past create voids in us.

In my case, it was the lack of a father figure. To make a very long story short, I was raised by a single mother of two girls. My father was never really around because he was in and out of jail my whole life. So, I grew up not knowing what the love of a father was. That created a void in me. A void is formed by a lack of something. This led me towards a promiscuous life. I was seeking the love of a man in different men. I wanted to be loved. Sex was my go-to whenever I felt down but it was only a temporary fulfillment. This void also made me very vulnerable to men and it led me to falling quick for any man. This is how my life went down the path of promiscuity.

Since I was lacking a father figure, I did not know how a man was supposed to treat a woman. I allowed men to treat me any way. I remember meeting this man in 2004 or 2005. I got into a relationship with him without getting to know him well. Just because he was treating me well on dates. I thought I knew him but I was wrong. As time went on, he became abusive. Everything was good the first year. But in the second year, he began to change. He became very possessive, obsessive, verbally abusive, some physical abuse occurred, jealous, manipulative and angry. It was a very toxic relationship that I did not know how to get out of.

He would always manipulate me and threatened to kill himself if I didn't want to be with him. This happened for almost 4 years. I finally sought help and lost the fear and walked away. It took so much but I did it! These are the things we run to, to complete us when we do not know God. We seek to fill our voids with the wrong things. When in all reality, it is God that completes us. For eternity!

One of the enemy's main schemes against us is to use our past to cripple us and keep us in bondage. This happens when we seek temporary things to fill that empty void we have. For example, in my case, I lacked a father figure my whole life and the enemy used that to make me attached to men. Just because I needed that affection. I needed a man to 'show' me and tell me that I was loved. If I didn't hear these words than I would feel rejected. Rejection was something I always battled with because of my past. The enemy knows this and uses things like this to harm us and make us feel like we are not loved. When we battle things, even how we react to certain things, stems from our past / childhood. In order for us to be victorious in winning that battle we first need to know who God is so that we may know who WE are in Him. And secondly, we must ask God to show us the root of the problem. He will tell us and He will heal us. But we must allow Him to. It's important to go back to our past no matter how painful it is so that we may be healed. It's a long process but definitely one that is needed in this walk. If we do not allow God to heal us, we will never be able to walk in full potential in the purpose that God has for our lives. We will become stagnant and we will not grow. God wants to heal us! What the enemy also does is that he will make things or people seem good for us so that we may fall into the trap. This is because he is a deceiver. He seeks to deceive us and destroy us. This is what happened to me. Many times I fell into a cycle of toxic relationships over and over again. This is because I was looking for 'love' in all the wrong places. The enemy knows what I was lacking and how I 'liked' them. So he made sure that he would paint it really nice, exactly how I wanted it. And BOOM! I was deceived! I didn't know God so therefore, I didn't know any better. This is why it became a cycle. Until God came through and broke that chain that was holding me back.

You're about to find out the exact reason you are here. Are you ready to discover your purpose in life?

Chapter Ten

WHY DID GOD CREATE US?

I'll never forget how amazed I was when I first found out how and why God created us. And to be honest, it still amazes me to this day! One question I always asked myself was, "Why was I born"? Have you ever asked yourself that question? Let me answer that for you. In Genesis 1:26 God said "Let us make man in our image, and our likeness: and let them have dominion over the fish of the sea, and over the fowl of the air, and over the cattle, and over all the earth, and over every creeping thing upon the earth." We were created in God's image and likeness. This means that we are to be like Him. I'm not saying to "Be God" and to 'look' like Him. But we are to think like Him, act like Him, and speak like Him. Of course this only happens after you begin to develop that personal relationship with God. The first humans God created were Adam and Eve. I'm sure you've heard this story many times over and over. God created Adam first and then from his rib, created the woman; Eve. He saw that the man was alone and said "Man shall not be alone so I'll create a woman for him". Long story short, they were placed in the Garden of Eden and were told by God that they were not to eat from the tree of knowledge of good and evil. Because if they did, they would die and their eyes would be open to bad and good. This is where free will began. Satan came as a snake, very subtle. And told Eve, "Did God really say that if you eat from this tree, you would surely die"? Deception began here. You can find this in *Genesis* but to summarize it a bit, Satan began to tell Eve that if she eats from the tree of knowledge of good and evil that she will know everything like God. She believed him and ate from the tree and even gave some to her husband, Adam. Once they both ate from the tree they realized that they were both naked so they hid from shame. They looked for figs to cover their nakedness. When God called them He'd asked them why they were hiding. And their reply was because they were naked and they heard Him. That's when God automatically knew that they had eaten from the tree He told them not to eat from. Although He already knew of course. He's God. This is when sin began. God gave them free will to choose AFTER He had already told them what to do and what not to do. But they still chose to disobey God for their desires. They desired the fruit because it looked delicious. They were deceived by Satan. This is when communion was lost between God and humanity. And this is why we are now living in a sinful world because there IS a devil that still deceives and there ARE people that still disobey God even when they know right from wrong.

God created us to serve Him, like I stated previously. It says in Matthew 5:16 "In the same way, let your light shine". And Exodus 23:25 says "You must serve only the Lord your God, if you do, I will bless you with food and water, and I will protect you from illness". We can serve God by serving others in need. When we meet the need of others, we are serving God. They begin to see God through our actions. And that's the point. So that God may get all the glory and honor and others may start to seek Him. Jesus was a servant! That is all He was about. The main reason you are here is to serve God. That is ALL our calling. That's why we are all here. We serve God with our gifts as well. Our gifts are given by God to be used for His glory. When we serve our churches, we are also serving God. When we serve our communities, we are serving God. When we are spreading the gospel, we are serving God. Everything that we do here on earth should be to honor God. We are also here to worship God. When God created Adam and Eve (the first humans), He created us to have communion with Him AT ALL TIMES! We were supposed to be able to talk with God and be in His presence. Face to face. But because of the disobedience that occurred in the Garden of Eden, sin broke that communion. There are many ways we can worship God. Tithing and offering is a form of worship to God. God doesn't care about the amount. He looks at the condition of your heart. We also worship God with our gifts. We praise with songs that will bring glory to His name. But there is one most important way to worship God, and that's with our lifestyle. The way we live. This is what God looks for. Sometimes we may say with our lips that we really honor and worship God but can we say that with our actions? Does our life reflect a life pleasing to God and can we say that we are obedient with the way we live? Who are we fooling right? Not God, that's for sure. We're only fooling others and most importantly, ourselves! Why am I writing this book? I need you to understand that God loves you even with your imperfections.

He created you and knew you before your own

mother ever did. That's mind blowing! He gave you your name. That name you have right now, He gave it to you. I need you to also understand who you were created to be. You were created for much more! Our human minds can never comprehend the things and plans God has for us. Please accept God's love today. I learned that many times we stay miserable and even be miserable Christians because we have a hard time accepting that God really does love us. God wants us to live free lives. Free for Him not free to have permission to do whatever we want. Once we come to God, we are supposed to feel freedom. Freedom from bondage, freedom from condemnation, freedom from judgement. Just free in Christ! I also need you to understand that if only you repent and turn away from your sins, you will be forgiven. God wants to forgive you. No matter what you've done. He specializes in turning beauty from ashes. He did it with me. This is why I am so convinced in what God can do for you. I know Him personally. He is our Father, our Friend, our Peace, our Strength, our Guide, our Comforter, our Husband, our Provider. And I can keep going on and on. God is who you allow Him to be in your life. Make Him your everything! You will not regret it. I anticipate in hearing testimonies on how good God has been to you! I always say that people go through things in life to help others in the long run. Our testimonies were never meant to be kept a secret. This is why I never stay quiet about the goodness of God. He has done so much in me, through me, and for me. And will continue to do so. And He will do the same for you! If you are reading this and have not accepted Christ as your Lord and Savior but you want to, before praying together I want to remind you of something. All God looks for in you, is a WILLING HEART. Nothing more. Do not be so hard on yourself and forget about the past. God tells you today, "Behold, I am making a NEW thing". Will you begin to LIVE today?

If you want Christ in your life, repeat this prayer out loud wherever you are. Even if it's in your heart. Say:

Prayer of Salvation

"Lord, today I heard about you and about your goodness. I open up my heart to you and receive you as my Lord and Savior. Thank you for dying on the cross for my sins. Help me to live a life pleasing to you. Please forgive my sins and write my name in the Book of Life and never erase it. Guide me in everything, show me who you are, and change me. Thank you for everything. In Jesus' name I pray, Amen"!

If you prayed this- CONGRATULATIONS! You are now saved and forgiven! Welcome to the family of God! Rejoice and know that you have received the Holy Spirit now that you are saved. The Spirit of God will help you in this walk. Just allow Him to and you will be just fine. And remember, you will NEVER be alone! You can now stop seeking elsewhere; you have found what was missing- God! And this is how you go from existing to living! Get ready to live a life of victory in God.